The Cutting Edge of Quantum Computing

Decoding the Puzzle

Table of Contents

Chapter 1. Introduction

Special Report: The Cutting Edge of Quantum Computing: Decoding the Puzzle

In our modern era of an ever-accelerating digital revolution, the enigma of quantum computing persists as an area both promising and perplexing. Fear not, this extraordinary special report, "The Cutting Edge of Quantum Computing: Decoding the Puzzle," is curated for your intellectual curiosity, distilling this complex subject matter into manageable, comprehensible nuggets. Travel with us through the labyrinth of qubits, superposition, and entanglement, as we demystify quantum computing's intricate workings. We navigate this cutting-edge field, highlighting its potential impacts on our world, from cryptography to AI, even as we maintain an anchor on what it means for individuals and organizations today. Whether you're keen on understanding the quantum hype, striving to keep abreast with technology, or aiming to grasp possible disruptions in your industry, this report is your comprehensive guide into the fascinating world of quantum computing.

Chapter 2. Quantum Computing: An Introduction

At its core, quantum computing is a new type of computation that leverages quantum mechanics to solve certain types of problems significantly faster than traditional computers can. To understand this revolutionary approach, let's unwrap the basic principles that underlie it, beginning from the science of quantum mechanics.

2.1. The Quantum World

Quantum mechanics, the science behind quantum computing, is a branch of physics that examines the world at a size below the level of atoms. It's a strange world down there, where particles can exist in two places at once or spin in opposite directions simultaneously, a phenomenon called superposition. Even more puzzling is entanglement, another quantum property where particles become linked together, such that the state of one can instantaneously affect the other, no matter the distance.

In the quantum realm, we have to abandon our daily intuitions based on classical physics. For instance, particles can exhibit wave-like behavior, duplicating themselves to pass through two slits at once. This odd behavior forms the bedrock of quantum mechanics and quantum computing, with the theory of 'wave-particle duality' playing a fundamental role.

2.2. Building Blocks: Qubits

Traditional computers use bits to process information, where each bit can be either a zero or a one. The magic of quantum computing, however, begins with the quantum bit, or qubit. A qubit is not just a zero or one; it can be both a zero and a one simultaneously, thanks to superposition.

A classical computer, given n bits, could be in one of 2^n states. Here, n bits are processed in parallel, creating a tremendous increase in computational speed. However, due to the rule of superposition, n qubits in a quantum system can be in any combination of 2^n states simultaneously, offering an exponential leap in computational power.

2.3. Superposition and Entanglement

As we have uncovered, a qubit can exist in multiple states at once due to superposition. This probabilistic nature is defined by a 'wave function,' a mathematical function that predicts all possible states of a quantum system. Upon measurement, the qubit collapses to one of its definite states, decided by the probabilities encoded in its wave function.

While superposition establishes a quantum system's multiple states, entanglement links these states together. Once qubits are entangled, a quantum state cannot be described independently of the others, even at significant distances. Einstein referred to this as 'spooky action at a distance.' The source of many quantum theories' counterintuitive nature, this correlation is what gives quantum computers their incredible computational speed and strength.

2.4. Quantum Gates and Circuits

In classical computing, logical operations are done using gates, and it's the same concept in quantum computing. However, quantum gates act on qubits and have special properties linked to the principles of superposition and entanglement.

Quantum gates manipulate the state of a qubit, creating complex calculations by combining these manipulations. Unlike classical gates, quantum gates are reversible by design. Furthermore, quantum gates maintain the coherence of the system, ensuring that superposition and entanglement remain unaffected until information is measured and read out.

Quantum circuits, composed of these gates and qubits, are the core components that deliver quantum algorithms.

2.5. The Quantum Computer

A quantum computer uses qubits, quantum gates, and quantum circuits, combined with the principles of superposition, entanglement, and quantum interference, to solve computations. First, through superposition, a quantum computer can process a vast number of possibilities simultaneously. Then, entanglement helps manipulate the superpositions, interconnecting qubits to create a vast web of probabilities. Finally, quantum gates and circuits systematically manipulate these quantum states to reach specific, optimized outcomes.

2.6. Advancements and Limitations

Quantum computers have the potential to resolve complex problems exponentially faster than classical ones, from simulating quantum systems in chemistry and physics to performing medical diagnostics and optimizing logistical operations.

Yet, there are substantial hurdles to overcome before quantum computers can be implemented on a practical scale. These include maintaining quantum coherence, managing the error rates in quantum cryptography, and hardware issues such as keeping the system isolated and at low temperatures.

Despite its complexities, this is an area of technology worth unravelling, with potential implications that may define the next technological revolution. Quantum computing is a computing paradigm shift like the transition from analog to digital, and our quest to decoding this puzzle could lead to advancements in technology that we can't currently fathom.

Chapter 3. Exploring the Quantum World: Key Principles

Quantum computing has always been difficult to grasp, primarily because it doesn't operate under the usual laws of physics that we are familiar with in our day-to-day lives. Rather, it adopts its rules from quantum mechanics, a branch of physics that describes the bizarre ways in which tiny particles like photons and electrons behave. So, to understand quantum computing, we must first delve into the key principles that form the quantum world.

3.1. Superposition

Superposition is a fundamental concept in quantum physics. A classical computer bit can only be in one state at a given time, either 0 or 1. On the contrary, quantum bits or qubits can exist in multiple states at once, thanks to the principle of superposition. A qubit can represent 0, 1, or any state in between - effectively, a qubit can be both 0 and 1 at the same time. This feature gives quantum computers their exponentially superior processing power.

The mathematical model of a qubit is represented by a sphere, called the Bloch sphere. On the surface of the sphere, the north and south poles typically represent the two extreme states 0 and 1, while points inside the sphere depict the superposition states.

3.2. Quantum Entanglement

Another fundamental characteristic of quantum mechanics is entanglement. This phenomenon links two particles in such a way that the state of one will instantly reflect changes in the state of the other, regardless of the distance separating them. This spooky action at a distance (as Einstein referred to it) allows quantum computers to work on many calculations simultaneously. It is crucial for quantum teleportation and quantum cryptography.

Albert Einstein was initially skeptical of entanglement, declaring it "spooky action at a distance". However, numerous experiments have verified its existence, and today it stands as one of the linchpins of quantum mechanics.

3.3. Quantum Tunneling

Quantum tunneling is another peculiarity of the quantum realm. It allows particles to pass through barriers that, in classical physics, would be insurmountable. This property is utilized in many quantum algorithms and has implications for the development of quantum computers.

In classical computing, a computer's transistor cannot switch until the electrons have a sufficient amount of energy to overcome the energy barrier. However, in quantum computing, the electrons "tunnel" through barriers, thus enabling faster data processing.

3.4. Quantum Decoherence

Decoherence is the loss of quantum behavior and is one of the significant challenges in building a useful quantum computer. When qubits interact with their environment, the superposition collapses, causing the qubits to behave like classical bits. The longer we wait, the more interoperability occurs, causing the loss of valuable quantum information.

To limit decoherence, quantum systems are often shielded from all possible forms of external interference. This process is challenging and has yet to be wholly achieved at a full, functional scale, thus putting a natural limit to the number of computations a practical quantum computer can complete. It is an area of ongoing research in quantum computing.

3.5. Quantum Gates

In a classical computer, logic gates are used to perform operations on bits. Similarly, in a quantum computer, quantum gates manipulate qubits. However, quantum gates are more complex due to the superposition and entanglement properties of qubits. A quantum gate can process numerous inputs simultaneously, thanks to superposition, while entanglement dramatically expands the potential outcomes.

Quantum computing also makes use of reversible gates, gates that can be reversed to get back to the initial state, given the final state. This principle is necessary because the laws of quantum mechanics are reversible. Notable quantum gates include the Hadamard gate and the Pauli-X gate, which perform base operations essential for quantum computation.

3.6. Quantum Algorithms

Quantum algorithms are designed to harness the power of quantum principles to resolve problems much faster than traditional algorithms. Quantum algorithms like Shor's algorithm for factorization and Grover's for searching display the genuine power of quantum computing. By exploiting the quantum properties of superposition and entanglement, they can solve problems faster than classical algorithms.

A successful implementation of these algorithms would profoundly impact several areas such as cryptography, which largely relies on the difficulty of factoring large numbers. Fast factorization by a quantum computer could break most existing cryptosystems, hinting at the revolutionary changes that quantum computing can bring to our world.

While the idea of quantum computing may stun our imagination, developing a full-scale quantum computer is still an objective of the future. To realize this goal, we must overcome several technical challenges. However, understanding the alluring principles of quantum physics that underpin quantum computing offers us a glimpse into the power and potential of this next-generation computing paradigm. Even as we stand at the cusp of quantum computing becoming a reality, it is fascinating how these principles that govern the micro world might soon reshape our macro world.

Chapter 4. Qubits and Quantum States: The Building Blocks

Quantum Computing's revolution, set to redefine our understanding of complex computations, begins with two foundational building blocks: qubits and quantum states. This journey explores these distinct, yet interconnected facets of quantum computing which bestow upon the field its distinctive characteristics and endless potential.

4.1. Qubits: Beyond Binary

The term qubit, short for "quantum bit," harks back to the fundamental building block of classic computing: the binary digit or bit. In traditional computing, bits are the smallest unit of data, with every bit taking either a 0 or 1 value - an on or off state. However, qubits transcend this rigid dichotomy.

A qubit, like its classical counterpart, can assume either a 0 or 1 state, but it can also exhibit both states simultaneously. This property - dubbed superposition – is a bedrock of quantum mechanics and one of the most perplexing. As the physicist Richard Feynman famously said, "If you think you understand quantum mechanics, you don't understand quantum mechanics." However, in relation to qubits, we can simplify the concept.

Imagine a sphere: on the classical bit level, you would place a mark either at the north or south pole, symbolizing a 0 or 1 value. A qubit, conversely, can conceive marks anywhere on the sphere surface, not only at the poles. This flexibility represents the potential states a qubit can take, powered by superposition.

4.2. Superposition: Multiplicity of States

Superposition, then, is the concept that revolutionizes our perception of data storage and computation, enlarging the scope previously constrained by binary digits. Qubits in a superposition can store an enormous amount of information compared to conventional bits. Moreover, they allow for parallel computations, thereby promising exponential speed up in certain problems.

Conceptually, a qubit in superposition exists in all its possible states until measured. The act of measurement, according to quantum mechanics, "collapses" the qubit into one of its basic states, either 0 or 1. Notably, the measurement outputs are determined probabilistically, not deterministically, unlike classical bits.

Imagine a coin spinning in the air. It is simultaneously in a heads-up and a tails-up state until it lands. Similarly, a qubit represents both states until we observe (measure) it. However, unlike the 50-50 chance of heads or tails in a tossed coin, qubit probabilities may not be evenly distributed. Crucially, quantum algorithms can manipulate these probabilities.

4.3. Quantum Gates: Control of Qubit States

Manipulating qubits from one state to another works via quantum gates, a close relative of the classical gates employed in regular computer circuits. Quantum gates, however, exploit quantum mechanical phenomena like superposition and entanglement, choreographing them to the benefit of quantum computation.

Key quantum gates include Pauli gates, Hadamard gate, CNOT gate, and many more. Each interacts with qubits in a unique manner:

some flip the states, some allow superposition, others create entanglement. Algorithms, at their purest, are sequences of these gate operations designed to solve particular problems.

Quantum gates operations are reversible, unlike classical gates. For instance, in classical binary, transforming a 1 to a 0 via a NOT gate is irreversible. However, in quantum computing, a series of state changes is always reversible up to the original status, allowing for a potentially phenomenal reduction in computational errors.

4.4. Entanglement

The second pillar of quantum mechanics, which takes qubits to another level, is entanglement - a phenomenon allowing particles to become instantaneously connected, regardless of their physical separation. When qubits are entangled, the state of one qubit becomes tied to the state of another. Any action on one qubit will immediately change the state of its entangled partner, even if they're galaxies apart.

Entanglement is not only central to quantum computation speedups but is also essential for quantum error correction techniques, enhancing the stability of quantum processors. Its non-locality characteristics further hint at potential breakthroughs in quantum communications and cryptography.

Each day, fresh insights into qubits, superposition, quantum gates, and entanglement offer glimpses into the vast potential of quantum computing. As we're only scratching the surface of these enigmatic yet intriguing building blocks, the promise of quantum computers propelling us into a new era of computational power is rapidly gaining momentum. As we dig deeper and uncover the complexities cloaked in this scientific arena, we may finally unlock the potential to tackle problems too immense or infeasible for classical computers.

Our journey doesn't end here, as the layers of qubits and quantum states continue to unravel their mysteries. Understanding these fundamental concepts, while complex, can guide us toward the heart of quantum computing: the quest for faster, more efficient, and consequently, more densely packed information processing in the digital age. Remaining apprised in this fascinating domain is integral to embracing the inevitable tide of quantum computing, destined to steer our digital destinies.

Chapter 5. The Enigma of Superposition and Entanglement

To truly understand quantum computing, an exploration of two fundamental concepts is indispensable: superposition and entanglement. These remarkable phenomena undergird the enormous potential and unparalleled capability of quantum computing.

5.1. Understanding Superposition

The concept of superposition in quantum mechanics defies our intuition shaped by classical physics. In the classical model, a bit can exist in two states, represented by 0 and 1. However, a quantum bit, known as a qubit, works differently, and here, the magic of superposition comes into play. A qubit can exist in both states—0 and 1—at the same time.

To make sense of this conundrum, imagine spinning a coin. While the coin is in the air, you cannot determine whether it will land heads or tails. During the spin, in a certain abstract sense, it is both heads and tails at once. This is analogous to a qubit in superposition. Of course, once you measure the coin's state—once it lands—it can only be either heads or tails. Analogously, a qubit, upon measurement, falls into a determinate state of being either 0 or 1.

The unique aspect of a qubit's superposition is that it is not a probabilistic 50:50 state, rather it exists in a precise state determined by the coefficients—known as amplitudes—attached to it, akin to a weighted lottery. The actual state of a qubit upon measurement is proportionally dependent on the square of these amplitudes. This feature of superposition is key to enhanced compute potential in quantum systems, enabling them to perform many calculations concurrently.

5.2. Quantum Entanglement

Quantum entanglement is another foundation pillar of quantum computing that sets it apart from classical computing. This phenomenon refers to how pairs or groups of particles can interact in ways such that the state of each particle cannot be described independently of the state of the others, even when particles are separated by a large distance.

The significance of entanglement is that it creates a deep link between particles, establishing a synchrony that exists no matter the expanse separating them. Picture having two entangled dice: when rolled, no matter the distance between them, if one comes up as a six, you instantaneously know the other is also a six. This is not due to any form of communication between the dice but rather is a result of the entangled state they were prepared in. The interesting part is: prior to measurement, both die outcomes were undetermined, yet correlated.

This feature provides a remarkable capability for quantum computing. By entangling qubits, quantum computers may process a vast number of computations simultaneously, thus exponentially expanding computational power unattainable by classical computers.

5.3. Superposition and Entanglement as Building Blocks

Both superposition and entanglement are crucial building blocks for quantum computing. The computing power of quantum computers relies heavily on the ability to generate and maintain these states. Therefore, understanding these sometimes-counterintuitive theories is key to appreciating the profound power latent within quantum computing.

Using these building blocks, quantum algorithms have been developed that can theoretically solve certain problems much more efficiently than classical computers. These problems span areas such as cryptography, optimization, and drug discovery, holding promise for a quantum leap of advancements in various industries if quantum supremacy is reached.

5.4. Quantum Gates and Their Role

On a practical level, the traits of superposition and entanglement take life through the use of quantum gates, the basic operations in quantum computing. Unlike classical gates that perform operations on classical bits and have defined outputs, quantum gates manipulate the state of qubits by changing their amplitudes, phases, and entanglements. They do so without collapsing the superimposed and entangled systems into a single state, thus preserving the quantum computational advantage.

The set of amplitudes defining the state of a qubit pre- and post-quantum gate operation can be described by matrices and vector algebra. Therefore, quantum computing often relies on advanced mathematical descriptions and principles, making it a complex, yet intriguing branch of computer science.

Moreover, simulating the result of quantum gate operations on entangled qubits is exponentially hard on classical computers, which further accentuates the quantum advantage.

5.5. Current and Future Challenges

Despite the immense potential quantum computers present, realizing their capabilities presents a profound challenge. Physical qubits are extremely fragile, with superposition and entanglement easily perturbed by environmental elements. Current quantum systems are characterized by high error rates. Hence, developing methods to create stable, error-free quantum computers is a critical ongoing research effort.

The notion of quantum error corrections and fault-tolerant quantum computing is the subject of intensive research. These areas could offer solutions to the present instability issues, opening the door to powerful, real-world quantum computing.

Moreover, the creation and management of multi-qubit entanglement across large quantum systems pose significant challenges. While these challenges are substantial, overcoming them is key for quantum computers to truly outcompete classical computers.

Finally, programming quantum computers and building quantum algorithms necessitate mastering complex mathematical concepts and a whole new programming paradigm. Such barriers make quantum computing a field at the cutting edge of both theoretical and applied research.

In conclusion, superposition and entanglement give quantum computers their unique dimensions of power and complexity. These idiosyncrasies are the source of both the immense promise and the challenging puzzles that quantum computing offers. Researchers continue to delve deep into these mysteries, hunting for breakthroughs that may usher in a new age of computing.

Chapter 6. Quantum Gates: Directing Quantum States

Quantum computers, unlike classical computers that use bits (values of 0s and 1s) as their unit of data processing, operate using quantum bits or 'qubits'. Qubits can exist in states of 0, 1, or both simultaneously thanks to a concept called superposition. This ability of qubits to exist in multiple states at once is what potentially allows quantum computing to perform calculations much faster and more efficiently than classical computers. However, in order to manipulate these qubits, certain devices are utilized, known as quantum gates.

6.1. The Basics of Quantum Gates

Quantum gates are the basic building blocks in the architecture of a quantum computer. They are operations that can change the state of qubits, leading to the probability-based outputs that make quantum algorithms incredibly powerful. Unlike classical logic gates (AND, OR, NOT, etc.), quantum gates are reversible and don't rely on binary logic. Instead, they operate on the principles of quantum mechanics, chiefly, superposition and entanglement.

A quantum gate takes one or several qubits as input and turns them into one or several qubits output. Quantum gates can be represented mathematically as matrices and the action of a quantum gate on a qubit is a simple multiplication of the gate's matrix with the vector representing the qubit's state.

6.2. Fundamental Quantum Gates

There are numerous types of quantum gates, however, some of the most fundamental ones include the Pauli gates, the Hadamard gate, and the Phase gate.

6.2.1. Pauli Gates

The Pauli gates are a group of three gates: Pauli-X, Pauli-Y, and Pauli-Z gates.

- The Pauli-X gate rotates the qubit's state around the x-axis by pi radians. Essentially, the Pauli-X gate is the quantum equivalent of a NOT gate in classical computing as it flips the state |0> to |1> and state |1> to |0>.

- The Pauli-Y gate also flips |0> to |1> and |1> to |0>, but it does so by applying rotations around both the x and z-axes.

- The Pauli-Z gate doesn't flip the qubits but rather changes their phase. It leaves the |0> state untouched but applies a phase of pi to the |1> state.

6.2.2. Hadamard Gate

The Hadamard Gate (H gate) is significantly critical in quantum computing as it generates superposition. The H gate transforms the basis state |0> to (|0> + |1>)/sqrt(2) and the basis state |1> to (|0> - |1>)/sqrt(2). It essentially creates a 50-50 chance of being in state |0> or state |1>, when a measurement is made.

6.2.3. Phase Gates

Phase gates are used to modify the phase of qubits. They include the S gate and T gate. The S gate applies a pi/2 phase to the |1> state and leaves |0> as it is. The T gate applies a pi/4 phase to the |1> state and leaves |0> unchanged.

6.3. The Act of Quantum Entanglement

Of all the quantum gates, controlled gates play a crucial role in the creation of a uniquely quantum phenomenon - entanglement. The most common of these gates is the controlled-NOT (CNOT) gate.

The CNOT gate operates on two qubits: a control qubit and a target qubit. If the control qubit is in state |1>, it flips the state of the target qubit. Interestingly, if the control qubit is in a superposition state, you'll end up with entangled qubits at the end of this operation.

Entangled qubits represent a drastic departure from classical systems, where the state of one particle becomes correlated with the state of the other, no matter the distance between them. This phenomenon, while notoriously difficult to comprehend, is a bedrock of quantum computing and quantum information science.

6.4. Working with Quantum Gates

All quantum gates can be described as rotations on the Bloch Sphere. The Bloch Sphere is a useful geometric visualization of the state of a single qubit: the poles of the sphere represent the two basis states, |0> and |1>. Superpositions of these basis states correspond to points on the sphere. Each quantum gate corresponds to a certain rotation.

While we've discussed a few fundamental gates here, a full quantum gate set—necessary to perform any arbitrary quantum computation—includes a variety of many more unique gates, often combining these basic ones in new and complex ways.

Importantly, error rates in executing quantum gates are a key benchmark for quantum computing capabilities. Reducing these errors and handling issues such as 'quantum decoherence' are vital steps in the practical application of quantum computing.

In conclusion, quantum gates are central to the functioning of quantum computers, and through the laws of quantum mechanics, they present a whole new paradigm in computational power. Their potential impact is earth-shattering, from breaking current encryption standards to accelerating the development of new drugs, to solving intractable computational problems. By understanding them, we stand at the threshold of a new technological era. Today, we are only scratching the surface of potential applications and implications.

As we continue to refine our understanding and improve our control over quantum gates, we hold the key to unlock the vast and largely untapped power of quantum computing.

Chapter 7. Quantum Algorithms and Their Applications

Quantum algorithms are the infrastructure that leverages the unique properties of quantum computing to solve complex problems efficiently. These algorithms are exponentially faster than classic algorithms, allowing quantum computers to handle tasks so enormous and complex that they're simply beyond the reach of classical machines. While Shor's algorithm, for factoring large numbers, and Grover's algorithm, for searching unstructured databases, are well-known examples, countless other algorithms are continually being developed in this rapidly evolving field.

7.1. Understanding Quantum Algorithms

Quantum algorithms are unique due to their employment of quantum bits, or 'qubits'. These are quantum analogues of classical bits but with powerful differences. Classical bits constitute data as 0s and 1s, essentially an either-or scenario. However, qubits, through a property called superposition, can exist as 0, 1, or any combination of both simultaneously. This core ability allows quantum computers to perform many actions at once, offering a significant speed advantage.

Quantum algorithms also exploit the phenomenon of quantum entanglement, where the state of two qubits are intrinsically linked, causing one to immediately reflect any changes made to the other, regardless of distance. This characteristic is leveraged to create complex correlations and perform intricate computations.

In a classical circuit, gates are used to modify the values of bits. Similarly, in a quantum setting, quantum gates alter the state of qubits. But unlike classical gates, quantum gates allow a wide range of transformations, enhancing computation diversity and capability.

7.2. Types of Quantum Algorithms

One can broadly categorize quantum algorithms into four types: Quantum Simulation, Quantum annealing, Quantum walk, and Quantum Fourier Transform algorithms.

1. Quantum Simulation algorithms are designed to mimic and predict quantum systems' behaviors, tasks that are naturally challenging for classical computers due to the complexity of quantum physics.

2. Quantum annealing algorithms are heuristic-based and are known for solving optimization problems. They exploit the natural tendency of quantum systems to find their ground state, the state of lowest energy, particularly relevant in materials science and AI.

3. Quantum walk algorithms are quantum counterparts of random walk models in classical physics, using the principles of superposition and entanglement to process information.

4. Quantum Fourier Transform algorithms, like Shor's, are heavily used in number theory and cryptography. They exploit the faster quantum version of the classical Fast Fourier Transform.

7.3. Prominent Quantum Algorithms

Let's delve into the specifics of well-established quantum algorithms, offering an in-depth understanding of their operations and potential applications.

1. Shor's Algorithm: Developed by Peter Shor in 1994, it is well

recognized for its ability to factor large numbers more efficiently than the best-known classical algorithms. Its potential ability to break RSA encryption, commonly used for securing online transactions, has made it a subject of great interest.

2. Grover's Algorithm: This algorithm, discovered by Lov Grover in 1996, performs unstructured searches exponentially faster than classical algorithms. It shows promise in numerous applications, including database management and machine learning.

3. Quantum Phase Estimation (QPE): QPE is one of the most fundamental quantum algorithms. It is critical to many quantum subroutines, including quantum simulation, advanced quantum algorithm designs, and foundational quantum error correction protocols.

7.4. Applications of Quantum Algorithms

Quantum computing, through its powerful algorithms, can potentially revolutionize various industries.

1. Cryptography: With the power of Shor's algorithm, quantum computers could break current cryptographic systems, compelling the quest for quantum-resistant cryptography.

2. Machine Learning and AI: Quantum machine learning algorithms can handle large datasets more efficiently, improving the accuracy of predictions and models while reducing computational time.

3. Drug Discovery and Healthcare: Quantum algorithms can accurately simulate molecular structures, accelerating the discovery of new drugs and furthering personalized medicine.

4. Logistics and Supply Chain: Quantum optimization algorithms can manage complex logistics problems, optimizing supply chain routes, and effectively managing tasks.

Although quantum computers that can fully harness these algorithms are still under development, the potential impacts of such technology are considerable. As we pave the way towards this new computing paradigm, understanding and exploring these quantum algorithms will be an instrumental part of the journey.

In summary, quantum algorithms are the workhorses of the quantum computing world, built upon the principles of superposition, entanglement, and quantum gates. Their development is rapidly evolving, and their potential applications across various industries make them an area of heavy investment and research, standing at the forefront of the quantum revolution.

Chapter 8. Quantum Computing vs Classical Computing: A Comparative Analysis

Today's computing landscape is dominated by classical computers that have served us well for decades. However, a paradigm shift is on the horizon, one being led by quantum computers, potentially capable of tackling problems beyond the reach of classical computers.

Let's embark on a comparative journey, analyzing the intricacies, differences, and advantages of quantum and classical computing.

8.1. Classical Computers: The Binary Titans

At the heart of every classical computer lies the binary code – strings of zeros and ones known as bits. They're the fundamental building blocks upon which all computations are based, residing in a definite state of either 0 or 1.

A classical computer processes these bits using logical gates that manipulate the bit's state through a set of rules. Instructions are processed sequentially, and performance escalates through increasing processing speed and miniaturizing the hardware, a trend famously known as Moore's Law. Over the past 50 years, this law has held true, but signs are showing it's coming to a plateau. Physics imposes a limit on how much we can miniaturize a transistor.

8.2. Quantum Computers: The Qubit Revolution

Quantum computers recast the classical computing blueprint. They employ quantum bits, or qubits, that leverage quantum phenomena. Unlike classical bits, qubits exist in a superposition, meaning they can be both 0 and 1 simultaneously.

This potentiality gives quantum computers the ability to solve multiple calculations simultaneously. Two qubits could represent four states simultaneously, three could represent eight, and so on, giving quantum computers a potential exponential growth in processing power.

Qubits are also subjected to an entanglement principle. If two qubits are entangled, the state of one qubit is instantly correlated with its pair, irrespective of any physical distance separating them. Manipulating one qubit would instantaneously affect the other, allowing quantum computers to process complex calculations almost instantaneously.

8.3. Making sense of Superposition and Entanglement

Superposition and entanglement are uniquely quantum phenomena that offer unprecedented computing power. However, they also represent new challenges, particularly in terms of error correction and consistency in results.

In a quantum computer, a qubit in superposition can iterate multiple computations simultaneously. Then, the quantum state collapses into a single answer when measured. The result, however, isn't deterministic like in classical computing but probabilistic, meaning we can only predict the probability of each result.

Entanglement furthers these difficulties. While it allows faster computation, it also makes error correction a significant challenge. One error can cascade through the entire system due to the interconnectedness of the qubits.

Such challenges aren't present in classical computers where bits are solitary entities, unaffected by the states of their neighbors.

8.4. Quantum Computing: Victories and Challenges

Quantum computers hold the potential to solve problems from different disciplines that would be time-consuming or entirely infeasible for classical computers.

For example, quantum computing could revolutionize the field of cryptography, making certain encryption standards obsolete while introducing new, impenetrable ones. Moreover, it could significantly accelerate drug discovery, weather prediction, and financial modeling.

However, they face major obstacles. The current technology for maintaining the stable quantum state is fleeting and error-prone, demanding exceptional environments with ultra-low temperatures and minimal disturbance. Furthermore, quantum algorithms are a new field with few experts and insufficient development tools.

8.5. Bridging the Gap: Quantum Supremacy

Google's quantum computer, Sycamore, achieved a key milestone, termed as 'quantum supremacy', by performing a calculation that would take a classical supercomputer an estimated 10,000 years, in just 200 seconds. This marked an exciting transition from quantum theory to practical application.

Yet, it's critical to remember that this was a specially-designed case and we're far from a universal quantum computer that can outperform classical ones on multiple arbitrary tasks.

8.6. The Future Intersection of Quantum and Classical Computing

While quantum computing's power is potentially vast, it's unlikely to replace classical computing altogether. Rather, they will coexist, each solving the problems they're most efficient at. Quantum computers might become tools for specialists in high-performance computing centers, dedicated to tackling specific tasks, while classical computers would serve everyday tasks where they're far more efficient and cost-effective.

As we continue to gain a better understanding and control over the quantum world, this still-nascent field reveals tantalizing glimmers of its future potential. Today, we are witnessing not a replacement, but a quantum leap in computational power, volatility, and potential. The lines between quantum and classical computing represent fertile grounds for exploration and innovation, with each advancement inching us closer towards a paradigm shift in computing power and potential. The quantum advantage is not just imminent but evolving into reality.

In this comparative exploration, we have unlocked the intricate fundamentals of both classical and quantum computing, probing their core components, their unique buzzwords, their victories, and their challenges. And while there is much we don't yet know about quantum computing, what is indisputably clear is that both classical and quantum will continue to wield significant influence in shaping our world.

Chapter 9. Revolutionizing Industries: The Power of Quantum Computing

Quantum computing is gaining excitement and also skepticism from a few, primarily because it offers the potential to redefine numerous sectors of industry and society at large. We delve into this potential in some detail in this chapter.

9.1. Financial Services

For the financial industry, quantum computing provides a new dimension to risk management, data analysis, and fraud detection. Portfolio optimization, a complicated task heavily dependent on probability and combinatorics can immensely benefit from quantum computing. Similarly, complex derivatives pricing and high-frequency-trading can also be dramatically improved owing to the sheer computational speed delivered by quantum systems. Anticipating the game-changing potential, banks like JPMorgan and Barclays have already established partnerships with quantum computing companies. However, a larger scale and a favorable regulatory environment are needed before quantum computing can become an industry standard.

9.2. Healthcare and Pharmaceuticals

In the healthcare and pharmaceutical sectors, quantum computing can lead revolutionary changes. Drug discovery can be significantly accelerated as it primarily revolves around computational chemistry — a prime candidate for quantum advantage with its ability to factor in all variables simultaneously while processing molecular simulations. Quantum algorithms can be used to model biochemical reactions, which are essential in understanding human cell metabolisms and root causes of specific diseases, such as cancer, Alzheimer's, and COVID-19.

9.3. Supply Chain and Logistics

Quantum models hold great prospects in optimizing complex logistics and supply chain scenarios. With quantum computing, companies can better predict demand, optimize routes, manage inventories, and crucially decrease operational costs. A key challenge in logistics — the famous 'traveling salesperson problem' — which includes finding the shortest visiting route for multiple cities, can be solved exponentially faster with quantum computing.

9.4. Energy and Climate

In energy and climate sectors, quantum computing can play a key role. It can help optimize renewable energy use and increase efficiency in minimizing greenhouse gas emissions. For example, it can help optimize grid management by balancing supply and demand in real-time, enabling a more effective use of renewable energies. It can also expedite the design of new materials for efficient energy conversion and storage.

9.5. Cybersecurity

Quantum computing has the potential to disrupt current encryption methods, making them obsolete. This stands to redefine the cybersecurity landscape, forcing a re-engineering of most existing encryption algorithms. However, the same superposition and entanglement that can potentially break traditional cyphers can also provide an opportunity to create 'quantum secure' encryption techniques, thus leading to a new security paradigm and practices.

9.6. Artificial Intelligence and Machine Learning

Artificial Intelligence (AI) and Machine Learning (ML) are fields where quantum computing can potentially revolutionize current paradigms. The significant gain in processing power can accelerate machine learning algorithms, enabling quicker decision making and advanced pattern recognition. This could greatly influence AI developmental sectors like autonomous vehicles, predictive modeling, and natural language processing.

The potential power of quantum computing is undeniable, and its expected influence across industries is profound. As much as it provides opportunities for positive disruptors, it undeniably introduces an element of uncertainty and risk. A deeper understanding of the technology's potential, perils, and the ability to harness its power will define the leaders in the upcoming technological renaissance.

Our understanding of quantum computing is still in its nascent stages, and while we comprehend its power and potential, completely harnessing it still poses technological hurdles and ethical challenges. In the following chapters, we delve into these challenges, their impact, and also lay out strategies to meet them head-on.

Chapter 10. The Challenges and Limitations of Quantum Computing

In as much as we are excited about the prospects and breakthroughs in quantum computing, it is important to keep our feet planted on the ground and acknowledge that there are tangible barriers and challenges that scientists and engineers grapple with in realizing the full capacity of quantum computing. These stumbling blocks are what partly slow the transition from theory and experimental setups into functioning quantum computers.

10.1. Technological Hurdles

One main challenge pertains to the creation and maintenance of quantum states. Quantum computation relies on harnessing state superpositions of quantum bits or "qubits". As one may suspect, keeping an electron in a state of superposition is no child's play. Outside interventions, such as electric, magnetic, or even thermal interference, can all too easily disrupt the necessary quantum states. This sensitivity to interference or 'noise' from the environment is known as "decoherence". Scientists are working to combat this through the creation of fault-tolerant quantum computers and error-correcting codes.

Such profound sensitivity to environmental disturbances has implications for the physical infrastructure in which quantum computer systems are constructed and housed. Quantum computers must be shielded from all external electromagnetic interference, and whole systems must be cooled to close to absolute zero temperatures. These strict and demanding conditions compound the challenges associated with the design, construction and upscaling of quantum devices.

Another predicament intrinsically related to qubits is their circuitry. Quantum gates, the heart of quantum circuits, need to be fast in their operations yet slow when it comes to interactions with the environment - a decidedly delicate balance to strike. Engineering quantum systems that can maintain this balance is a continuing challenge.

10.2. Scaling Complications

Scaling quantum systems presents another class of concerns. Due to the fragile nature of the qubits and their state of superposition, building a large scale quantum computer is a formidable challenge. Each qubit added to the system exponentially increases its complexity and decreases its stability. Hence, the construction of a robust and fault-tolerant quantum computer with many qubits is a significant endeavour.

This whole process raises the issue of "quantum volume," a measure of the computational effectiveness of a quantum computer, reflecting the largest square-shaped quantum circuit of equal width and depth that can be run reliably on a quantum system. Quantum volume takes into account not only the number of qubits but also the quality of the operations that can be performed. It illustrates how adding more qubits isn't always the answer if the coherence times, gate and measurement errors, crosstalk, and connectivity are not simultaneously optimised.

10.3. Practical and Theoretical Hurdles

On a more abstract, theoretical level, several mathematical and conceptual challenges remain unresolved. For instance, there's no general method for transforming a classical algorithm into a quantum one. This means that each time we want to utilise a quantum computer, we'll need to devise a new quantum algorithm from scratch.

Creating quantum programming languages that are easier to learn and use is another challenge. Current quantum programming often requires a deep understanding of quantum physics, which creates a high barrier to entry.

Meanwhile, there's also the issue of quantum speedup — the idea that a quantum computer can outstrip any classical computer. This premise is yet to be definitively proven in practice, with complex quantum processors necessary to test it.

And then, of course, there are the problems we can't predict yet. Any groundbreaking technology will face unknown hurdles. Quantum computing, as a pioneering and complex field of study, is likely to be laden with some surprises along the way.

10.4. Policy and Security Implications

Quantum computing also carries significant implications for cybersecurity. The advent of powerful quantum computers threatens the security of current encryption schemes. While progress is being made in the development of quantum-resistant cryptography, it's likely to be a protracted cat-and-mouse game between code makers and code breakers. Hence, the development of quantum technology policy frameworks that can keep up with the pace of change is a critical challenge.

Despite these challenges, however, the enthusiasm and optimism amongst researchers and developers remains high. It's a race of technological advancement where participants strive to unravel the complex secrets of atomic and subatomic particles, to solve complex problems, and perhaps to ignite the next technological revolution.

In quantum computing lies the potential to design drugs more efficiently, optimize logistics, enhance AI, improve weather prediction, and solve complex scientific problems. These rewards on the horizon continue to fuel the investments and the efforts in the development of quantum computers, driving ingenious solutions and approaches to tackle each of the obstacles on the daunting but promising quantum journey.

Chapter 11. Looking Beyond: The Future of Quantum Computing

Quantum computing remains in its infancy, with much of its potential yet to be realized. However, researchers and futurists have begun to forecast its influential role in the future. Here, we delve deeply into the prospective impacts of quantum computers, envisaging their transformative effect on various industries and arenas of society.

11.1. A New Dawn: Quantum Supremacy

One of the most anticipated milestones in quantum computing is achieving "quantum supremacy." The term refers to the point at which a quantum computer can solve a problem that no classical computer could feasibly resolve, even given a long timespan. Google made headlines in 2019 when it claimed its quantum processor solved a complex mathematical problem in just over three minutes, a task that would reportedly take the world's fastest conventional computer approximately 10,000 years. While the debate about whether true supremacy was achieved persists, it nonetheless signaled an indication of the massive computational leap quantum technology could bring.

11.2. Disrupting Current Security Paradigms

Given their unprecedented computational capabilities, quantum computers jeopardize current encryption methodologies, potentially exposing our digital security systems as obsolete. RSA encryption, a cornerstone of modern cybersecurity, relies on a computer's inability to factorize large prime numbers—a task a quantum machine could perform in mere moments. As we approach the era of quantum prevalence, a new chapter in cybersecurity, 'Post-Quantum Cryptography,' is unfolding. The focus here will be on building algorithms that can withstand quantum-enabled attacks, ensuring that our digital world remains safe and secure.

11.3. Transforming Artificial Intelligence and Machine Learning

Artificial Intelligence (AI) and Machine Learning (ML) stand to gain significantly from quantum computing. Quantum machines can perform extensive calculations rapidly, perfect for the data-heavy requirements of AI and ML applications. Quantum computing may enable faster, more accurate predictive modeling and larger, more complex neural networks—profoundly optimizing the processes of machine learning and, by extension, AI.

11.4. Revolutionizing Drug Discovery and Healthcare

The potential applications of quantum computers in healthcare and bioinformatics are profound. By mapping and analyzing molecular structures and interactions, quantum machines could expedite drug discoveries, personalized medicine, and genomics research. The multi-faceted computational needs of biological systems would be beneficially paired with quantum computing's parallel processing capabilities, potentially leading to holistic, novel approaches to healthcare.

11.5. Shaping Climate Modeling and Sustainable Energy

Climate modeling and sustainable energy research, inherently complex and data-rich fields, can also significantly benefit from quantum technology. Simulating complex climate-related events or exploring the potential of new energy sources does strain classical computing's limits. Quantum computers, with their unique problem-solving approach, might provide the sophisticated modeling tools needed to address these global challenges.

11.6. Realizing Quantum Internet

The idea of a 'Quantum Internet' takes quantum computing to a new level, suggesting a network where quantum information is transmitted over long distances through quantum entangled particles. If realized, such a network would be secure, incredibly fast, and could open up a bevy of new technological advancements.

11.7. Consumerization of Quantum Computing

Though quantum computers are primarily viewed through an enterprise lens, we may eventually witness their consumerization. While this reality is likely many years away, innovations like quantum random number generation or personal quantum encryption could be part of the individual user's technological arsenal in the future.

Though the path ahead for quantum computing is replete with challenges—ranging from error correction to scalability—its potential transformative power is undeniable. It is this dual prospect of incredible breakthrough and significant disruption that shapes our view of a future quantum world—a journey peppered with the excitement of untapped possibilities. Irrespective of the path, our focus should remain steadfast on harnessing this technology for the betterment of humanity, whether that be in eradicating diseases, forging a sustainable future, or advancing our understanding of the universe itself. The future of quantum computing is both a thrilling proposition and a solemn responsibility. Only time will unravel this intricate story of human innovation. Still, one thing is certain—quantum computing, in its full-fledged form, will reshape the way we perceive and interact with the world.

www.ingramcontent.com/pod-product-compliance
Lightning Source LLC
LaVergne TN
LVHW051627050326
832903LV00033B/4690